Naked Marketing

Naked Marketing
*A journey to the future
of marketing*

by

J Christian Andersen
Relationwise A/S

NAKED MARKETING

info@relationwise.com

Tel.: (+45) 70 268 264

Cover art: Veselin Milacic
Illustrations: Georgia Knowles
Book design: Sabine Sørensen
Published by: Motus

Forlag: BoD – Books on Demand, København, Danmark
Fremstilling: BoD - Books on Demand GmbH - Norderstedt, Tyskland
ISBN: 9788771703733
First edition 2014

www.relationwise.com

Contents

Introduction

The Naked Emperor   7

Chapter 1

A Brief History of Advertising and its Inevitable Decline   15

Chapter 2

Transparency Makes the Façade an Illusion   29

Chapter 3

Frankenstein's Monster Looking for Love   47

Chapter 4

The Key to This Business is Personal Relationships   65

Chapter 5

#thischangestheworld   85

Conclusion

You are Naked Too 107

Postscript 117

Introduction

The Naked Emperor

Let me begin with the familiar fable of "The Emperor's New Clothes." As the story goes, one day the Emperor hired two weavers who promised him the finest and most regal suit of clothes. The fabric to be used was so exalted, it could not be seen by anyone who was either unfit for his position or was hopelessly stupid.

As soon as the Emperor endorsed the project, the swindlers began their work. They set up a state-of-the-art workshop that appeared to be busy with activity. Of course, no one in the castle could see the fabric the two were allegedly using, but no one said anything. It was not their place to do so, and no one wanted to admit to being stupid.

After making a show of working diligently and collecting their fat fee, the swindlers reported the costume was finished. They pretended to dress the Emperor, who proudly marched in procession before his subjects. The townsfolk played along with the pretence, not wanting to appear stupid or unfit for their positions. Then a child in the crowd, too young to understand the advantages of keeping up the pretence, blurted out that the Emperor was wearing nothing at all – he was naked. In short order, the Emperor was disgraced.

There was a time when consumers – just like the townsfolk – could be fooled by such a scam. But today, no company can hide behind flashy advertising and marketing. Sooner or later – maybe not in a parade, but on social media, or simply friends or colleagues talking to each other – a person will point and say, "This is all fake!"

This new paradigm is slowly seeing the daylight, and nowhere in the world is it stronger than in São Paulo, Brazil. In 2007 the city's business community had to face a new reality when all advertising in public spaces was banned. As you will find out, this act of "creative destruction" (a term coined by Joseph Schumpeter in 1942) pushed regional companies to rethink and innovate their marketing. In many ways, São Paulo represents the city of the future, and for us on the other side of the world it is a crystal ball through which we can look into the future and see what will soon become reality for the rest of us.

I had to experience the miracle of São Paulo for myself. Working with companies for years and always curious why some companies stand out of the crowd, I saw travelling to São Paulo as a compelling opportunity I couldn't miss. Equipped only with my computer, an open mind, and a journalist contact, I boarded a plane for São Paulo.

I had no idea where this journey would take me, but I was eager to find out.

In the pages of this book, you can share what I experienced on my trip to the southern hemisphere. Together we will visit four fascinating people. I chose them wisely and with a strong intuition that they could each bring new understanding and new insights to the challenge of marketing, and together they would form what would hopefully become a beautiful picture of the future. The four people are a professor, an ad agency executive, a marketing director, and finally a man who had designed a ground-breaking campaign for one of the biggest banks in South America, a campaign that pointed the way towards a new approach to marketing – one that aligns business with a progressive movement.

Connecting to Customers

In this book, we'll explore how marketing has become free-form, digital, and collaborative. What was once easy to define – a TV ad buy, for example – has become multi-faceted, more nuanced, and more connected to people's lives.

In the new world of naked marketing, there's no one-size-fits-all solution. But that's okay. What we need to remember is that at the end of the day, business is fundamentally *human*. Natural, human conversation is the true language of commerce, and corporations work best when the people on the "inside" make a sincere connection with the people on the "outside."

Evolving into naked marketing means going from *organisation* to *organism*. The system is organic. Rather than to compete against each other, people are increasingly motivated to collaborate and work towards collective goals. We embrace collaboration for new ideas and open-forum conversations that spark more "human" campaigns.

Because it's not what you learned in business school, you may be puzzled as you read this. But as you will soon find out, this is not theory; it's already reality.

Naked Marketing celebrates and outlines the non-deceptive tactics used to engage modern consumers – tactics modern consumers are beginning to expect. Today's consumers will no longer allow big media, corporations, or any other seller to lie to them. In terms of products, they want to understand exactly what they are sold and they want the marketing message to be honest. Increasingly, consumers also want the corporation – global giant or neighbourhood shop front – to reflect and embody their values and ideals. This comes with increased awareness of how companies conduct their business.

Consumers themselves are becoming more and more central to spreading the word about products. The word can be good, bad, or a combination of both. Consumers use the web to create links to content and social media applications shared between friends. Supercharged by the internet, the new digital forms of word-of-mouth are becoming increasingly powerful.

Gone are the days of a company acting as the singular voice of its brand in the marketplace. In a world filled with social media, blogs, email, texting, and the capability for any individual to voice his or her opinion about any brand through the use of these tools, a naked approach to your marketing is both a reality and a requirement.

In the pages ahead, I'll reveal how naked marketing can bring your organisation into alignment with today's powerful trends in customer engagement, and how this organic approach will lead to stronger growth and a healthier bottom line for your company.

Chapter 1

A Brief History of Advertising and its Inevitable Decline

It was spring in New York at the height of the Roaring Twenties. Thousands of spectators lined the sidewalks of Fifth Avenue, watching a parade. A group of fashionable women in flapper dresses and bobbed hair hidden under cloche hats walked in the parade. But unlike the crowd, they were not there just to celebrate. They were part of a publicity stunt staged by a rising young public relations man named Edward Bernays. He was the nephew of Sigmund Freud and, having read his uncle's work, was keen to learn whether the theories of psychology could be applied to the practice of mass marketing.

Why was Bernays involved in the Easter parade? Because the giant American Tobacco Company was having a hard time figuring out how to get more customers for its cigarettes. Since the booming of the industrial age, the problem was no longer mass-producing its products but creating more smokers.

At that time it was not acceptable for women to smoke in public. George Washington Hill, the president of the American Tobacco Company, realised that if he could make smoking attractive to women, he would have a vast number of new customers. A year earlier he had said, "It will be like opening a gold mine right in our front yard." To increase the number of women smokers, Hill hired Edward Bernays to find out how to develop the potential of this market.

Bernays wanted to create a sensation. He found the perfect opportunity in the annual New York Easter Parade, a gala social event. He appropriated the term "torches of freedom," which had been used by Abraham Arden Brill, the first psychoanalyst to practice in the United States, to describe the desire women felt to smoke in public. By linking the torch from the Statue of Liberty to women holding another torch – the cigarette – Bernays made it the clarion call of the tobacco industry. Who could be against freedom? And would the analogy work? In a carefully planned scheme that many would now say was highly cynical, Bernays hired the attractive women to march up Fifth Avenue in the Easter parade and publicly smoke their "torches of freedom." The planted smokers were filmed and photographed. Of course, the press had already been alerted to what was going to happen in advance – by Edward Bernays.

The images of the women smoking cigarettes were splashed across every newspaper in the country and in the newsreels shown in every movie theater. It was a new form of marketing campaign that no one had ever carried out before.

And it worked brilliantly.

As reported in the *Journal of the American Medical Women's Association*, in 1923 women only purchased five per cent of cigarettes sold. By 1929 the female market had increased to twelve per cent, and by 1935 women comprised over eighteen per cent of the cigarette market.

Edward Bernays became known as "the father of public relations," and was later chosen by *Life* magazine as among the one hundred most influential Americans in the twentieth century.

Clearly, the power of a carefully orchestrated advertising campaign had been proven – for better or worse. The age of modern marketing had begun and soon every company had learned about mass marketing.

The advertising industry that began nearly a century earlier had now become a social and cultural force.

Let's turn back the clock to see how it all began.

The Origins of Advertising

Meet Mr Volney B Palmer. The year is 1841. The place is Philadelphia, Pennsylvania. Mr Palmer is a gruff-looking man who, like many other hard-nosed businessmen of the time, is seeking a way to keep his commercial interests afloat. Among his many holdings is a small coal supply company. No doubt his product contributes to the choking haze that shrouds cities from London to San Francisco.

Volney Palmer is of interest to us for one reason: he is credited with operating the first successful advertising agency in the United States. His business plan was very simple: he bought large amounts of space in newspapers at discounted rates and then resold the space at higher rates to companies and individuals who wished to advertise a product or service.

Most of his advertisements were straightforward messages announcing the availability of a product, not unlike today's classified ads. The few lines of text gave the name of the product, the place where you could buy it, and the price. There were a few exceptions, most notably the patent medicine ads that made outrageous claims about curing every disease known to man. But generally, an advertising agency was no more than a *messenger* that delivered product information from the client to the audience.

To be fair, Palmer did not invent advertising; he helped turn it into an industry. Humans have long hawked their goods and services. As far back as 1759, Samuel Johnson had complained, "Whatever is common is despised. Advertisements are now so numerous that they are very negligently perused, and it is therefore become necessary to gain attention by magnificence of promises, and by eloquence sometimes sublime and sometimes pathetic."

For a product "to gain attention by magnificence of promises" – now that's something every consumer has experienced!

After the Second World War, consumer goods companies and the advertising industry exploded. It culminated in an endless stream of one-way communication that flowed from manufacturers through ad agencies to the growing middle class.

Consumers were barraged with billboards, TV ads, and radio ads. Not just consumer products but also business to business. And during the 1970s, companies started to use telemarketing as a way to reach more people.

In the 1970s consumers were exposed to about five hundred ads a day. Today, that has increased to an estimated *five thousand* a day. What would Samuel Johnson say?

Towards the end of the twentieth century, like a drug addict needing a bigger and bigger fix, the advertising and marketing people were starting slowly but steadily to destroy themselves. It was not just an American phenomenon. The companies screaming for attention had long since spread out to the rest of the world and very much indeed to "the New York of the tropics" – São Paulo, Brazil.

Creative Destruction

It's the 26th of September 2006. It seems like another normal day in São Paulo, where in its many office buildings sales and marketing managers are working hard to figure out new plans and campaigns to attract more customers and gain a new market share. It's selling by yelling. More and more phone calls need to be made, more and more ads need to be created. The competition is rough and they have to speak louder and louder to get people's attention.

If you look outside the office window you can see the results of the work done inside.

Fifteen thousand billboards cover the city. It's a visual cacophony, a chaotic mashup of colours and logos and images, each one promoting a product or service and giving the impression that this great city is nothing more than a scaffold for obnoxious advertisements. Vinicius Valvao, a reporter at *Folha de São Paulo*, Brazil's largest newspaper, said in an interview, "You could not even see the architecture of the old buildings, because all the buildings, all the houses were just covered with billboards and logos and propaganda."

And as the BBC said, "A remarkable number of ads feature giant images of men and women dressed only in their underwear, while the Brazilian edition of *Playboy* is publicised with huge posters and cut-outs of the latest centrefold models. It all adds to the sensory overload of a city that many see as South America's version of the hi-tech cityscape portrayed in the film *Blade Runner*."

At the same time in another office, a man is sitting with a plan. A plan that is going to send shock waves through the city. The man is mayor Gilberto Kassab, and from City Hall on that day he declares *Lei Cidade Limpa* – the Clean City Act.

In just three months, every billboard had to go.

The companies were shocked. How could they get new clients? Would they lose their existing clients?

Even many ordinary *Paulistanos* were worried, fearing that the city's grey concrete would look drab and boring without the generous splashes of colour provided by advertising. The BBC quoted one citizen as saying, "It would be like New York without Times Square." Another said, "No, it would be like Eastern Europe before the fall of communism."

On the streets of São Paulo, Mayor Kassab hoped to replace the overbearing signage with human-scaled "street furniture" – bus shelters, information panels, and kiosks like the ones in London or Paris.

The bill passed the city council and became law. On the first day of January 2007, the city woke up to a new reality.

The billboards were gone, and with them one of the traditional methods used by advertisers to get people's attention.

Whether it's billboards, banner ads on the computer, TV commercials, or telemarketing, these traditional methods all try to *interrupt* people as they go about their daily lives.

You're driving your car and suddenly a big billboard looms overhead – it's an interruption. The phone rings when a telemarketer calls – another interruption. You're watching your favourite show on TV and suddenly you see an ad for a fast-food restaurant – another interruption.

What if you were one of the sales and marketing people who were trying to interrupt the consumer and suddenly you couldn't advertise the way you used to? What if you couldn't make that cold call to a prospect like you used to? What if everything you did yesterday was not possible today? Maybe not because it was made illegal, but simply because the traditional advertising wasn't effective anymore?

In his theory of creative destruction, Joseph Schumpeter asserted that the essence of capitalism was that the emergence of new methods, industries, and products must be equally counterbalanced by the destruction of old ways that had been rendered useless or were an impediment to progress. The key to creative destruction is that for some segment of society – workers, consumers, owners – there will be pain. A society cannot reap the rewards of rebuilding without accepting that some individuals will be worse off, not just in the short term, but perhaps forever.

Throughout history, examples of the replacement of the old with the new abound. For example, take that ancient mode of human transportation, the horse. Horses were used by nearly everyone, everywhere – from pulling omnibuses in cities to hauling wagons on farms. In New York City by the end of the nineteenth century the streets were jammed with over 150,000 horses. The twenty pounds of manure produced daily by each beast resulted in more than three million pounds of horse manure per day that needed to be disposed of. That's not to mention the daily 40,000 gallons of horse urine. One New York prognosticator of the 1890s concluded that by 1930 the horse droppings would rise to Manhattan's third-story windows.

This huge army of horses – not only in New York, but in every city and town in America and Europe – supported a vast industry of blacksmiths, tanners, stable owners, carriage makers, feed suppliers, veterinarians, and horse breeders. According to *American Heritage Magazine*, in 1880 New York and Brooklyn were served by 427 blacksmith shops, 249 carriage and wagon enterprises, 262 wheelwright shops, and 290 establishments dealing in saddles and harnesses.

Then came the car – a classic example of creative destruction.

Cheap, fast, and increasingly reliable, "horseless carriages" quickly replaced horses on both city streets and country roads. By 1920, there were over eight million registered automobiles in the United States. The 1920s saw tremendous growth in automobile ownership, with the number of registered drivers almost tripling to twenty-three million by the end of the decade. Dozens of spin-off industries blossomed, including vulcanised rubber, petroleum, road construction, auto repair, gas stations, and parking lots.

While no city ever took such drastic action as banning horses completely from its boundaries, it was an inevitably change that was beyond regulations. By 1930, horses had nearly vanished from the streets of New York, with only the hansom cabs remaining for romantic rides around Central Park.

If you were in the horse business in 1900, within twenty years you had either changed your business or cashed out.

In São Paulo, the creative destruction of the billboard industry caused the billboard companies to suffer financial losses. Before the law took effect, critics worried that the advertising ban would entail a revenue loss of $133 million and 20,000 people would lose jobs. Schumpeter's enduring assertion reminds us that capitalism's pain and gain are inextricably linked. The process of creating new industries cannot advance without sweeping away the pre-existing order.

Whether or not you like the billboard ban – that's not the point – the city's edict was an act of creative destruction that forced companies to search for new solutions. The companies that were agile were the ones that adapted and prospered.

It seems like the time for creative destruction has come to the world of marketing, too.

Chapter 2

Transparency Makes the Façade an Illusion

The taxi sped up. Crossing this crowded city of twelve million people was no Sunday drive. Despite my driving fast on the superhighway, the urban sprawl didn't seem to end. I passed skyscrapers that looked as if they were built on other skyscrapers.

People were everywhere, and they came in all shades – white, brown, black. This rapidly growing metropolis is the largest city in the southern hemisphere and the world's eleventh largest city by population. It's a city of great contrasts – rich and poor, traditional and progressive, boastful and reticent.

I noticed there were no billboards, the shop signs were small, and the taxis were not covered with advertising.

No billboards – but in the sky above me swarmed countless helicopters. São Paulo is a city with an incredible number of helicopters.

In my quest for answers I thought I too would take a helicopter, for a great view. Well, at least metaphorically speaking.

I was en route to a meeting with Professor J C Rodrigues, who teaches at the most famous business school in São Paulo. Besides lecturing, he works for the Walt Disney Company in their Brazilian office.

An assistant ushered me into the Professor's office. It looked like a kid's room, with lots of different Disney toys and a Winnie the Pooh stuffed animal. He had three computers turned on. Sitting there smiling and welcoming me, he looked like The Nutty Professor.

After some small talk, I went directly to the big question: "What's the future of marketing?"

He leaned back in his chair and thought for a moment. "Good question! Since I started teaching at the university eleven years ago, I've been trying to find one common mindset for marketing. Today, the issue is not the migration away from mass marketing – there's still plenty of that – but the migration from *interruptive* to *non-interruptive* marketing.

"Five years ago, we were discussing the difference between online and offline. But look at YouTube. Now you have the pre-roll or introductory video before the video itself. That five- or ten-second advertisement is an example of old-fashioned *interruptive* advertising. That's the cancer of the offline media spreading to the online media.

"In my opinion this strategy – designed to make money for YouTube and the people who post their videos – is a throwback. We should not take the worst of offline advertising and try to apply it online. Instead, both online and offline should use the best forms of non-interruptive marketing. The billboard ban in São Paulo is interesting because there were multiple discussions on what would happen next, so there was not only the billboard ban and who would be losing money on that but what would come next. I want to communicate, but how can I do that and build my brand when I'm not allowed to interrupt anymore?

"In the past there was cable TV, and it did not have advertising on it. You paid for the cable TV because you didn't want adverts. But then they added the advertising, and people migrated to Netflix. Then there was a movement of people cutting their cable TV subscriptions, at least in the United States. Consumers decided to choose on-demand services, because then you don't need to see adverts.

"That's a behavioural change, and it's related to the São Paulo ban on billboards. And after all, it all comes to the same end. Interruptive communication is no longer working."

I told the Professor I had spoken to a local businessman in São Paulo who works in marketing, and he had said they really wanted the billboards back so he could start to promote his products. I asked him if he had measured the effects of the billboard ban, and how many new sales he would generate with billboards. He looked at me as if no one had asked him that question before. He admitted he didn't have a proper answer for that.

It's a story we have heard before. As John Wanamaker said more than one hundred years ago, "Half the money I spend on advertising is wasted. The trouble is, I don't know which half." He was considered by some to a proponent of advertising and a pioneer in marketing.

The Professor smiled and leaned forward in his chair. "Initially, the agencies had a lot of concern about this, because they would be losing this part of their marketing. I don't believe personally that a brand or an agency has missed anything on this. It was a change, a shock, a mindset change.

"It would have happened anyway. Even if we didn't have the billboard ban, the investment would have migrated to one-on-one, less interruptive forms of media. So it is kind of killing something that was already old and outdated."

Business–to–Business

"What's your perspective on business-to-business selling versus business-to-consumers in relation to the future of marketing?" I asked the Professor.

"What is interesting is that B2B does not really exist," he said. "It is people buying from other people, even if you are buying as a company. As a purchaser within a company, it is still a person buying something. How you market to other businesses isn't that much different from how you market to the general audience.

"You have perceptions and expectations, and you may or may not believe what the brand or company is saying to you. In our digitally connected world, consumers talk to each other; consequently brands are increasingly exposed and cannot rely on advertising to hide their failures or enhance or prove their benefits. They need to be more real and communicate what they are, and they need to *be* what they're communicating.

"If you consider that this is the premise for how you do business, once you have your foundation, your DNA, and it is not all marketing speech but a way of life, the way you do business and the way you talk to your customers and offer them benefits will turn from a one-way marketing communications speech to something that's a conversation. One additional benefit, by the way, is that your employees will be more deeply committed to the brand essence.

"It's a different form of marketing. You're not enhancing your benefits or hiding your failures. You're showing the people what you really are, and with that you bring forth the perception of the company itself.

"That's what they're trying to do by becoming more of a people-to-people rather than a business-to-business company. The businessman doesn't change his personality just because he returned to his family at five o'clock and takes his tie off."

We live in a world that embraces logic. In our professional lives, we think we use only reason. The latest research has revealed that the part of our brain that makes decisions about money and trade is the part whose primary task is to manage emotions. To make economic choices, we use a part of the brain that's designed for a different purpose. In many ways, the B2B and B2C distinction is completely outdated.

"When you talk about business people," continued the Professor, "trust is something that can trigger an emotion. For example, I need to feel secure that the company from which I bought a service or product will respond if I have problems, and that they will make me successful and make me look good in front of my colleagues. Trust will bring happiness, because you don't need to worry. It's an emotion, and companies and their people can create it. Maybe it's not the same emotion that you get with Disney movies, with people crying and laughing. But it is an emotion after all, and it creates the same value for the company. You'll continue doing business with the company because you trust them, and by trusting them you become happy because you don't have any issues to deal with."

Why Are We In Business?

"Let's change the subject," I said. "You're a teacher at the business school here, and if you read all the classic business books and the definition of a business, it's always about the shareholders and making money for the shareholders. Aren't those definitions old-fashioned? And what is the new definition?"

"I conduct an interesting experiment with my students," said the Professor. "I ask them, 'Why does this company exist?' The ultimate answer to that is, money! Of course, all companies exist to make money; that's obvious. But the difference is the question you get right after that: *Why* do you want to make money? It's not because the shareholders will make more money; that's too simplistic. But why do you want to do that? Why exactly do you exist? What is your purpose? If you are a person, why are you alive? How do you describe that? How can you help people?

"Here in Latin America, an Apple computer costs twice as much as a PC. Why do people pay the high price? Because the brand essence helps them to define themselves. There is meaning; there is a why. So it's more emotional than rational. They offer you something more than just the product. Ultimately, people will pay for that."

I said that it's funny that most companies seem to be afraid to talk about that. They hide themselves and use words such as "mission" and "vision."

The Professor nodded. "That's a problem with business today. The mission/vision concept is really strong but it has lost its real value. It has turned into a plague at the president's office. They are just words. It was strong once, and then when you put that in a beautiful frame, it does not represent what they are and it does not guide their decisions. So it is sad that the mission/vision concept is really strong and not necessarily something that is outdated. But they need to be what they initially intended to be.

"It is essential for any company to have this mission or vision. You can call it whatever you want: some brands call it 'brand essence,' others call it 'company DNA.' But it's something in which you must really believe; it cannot be merely fancy words in a fancy frame. What a lot of companies do not understand is that they have the slogans and other forms of advertising, and they may have the mission/vision, but these are not things that help them to make decisions. To have any meaning, their mission/vision must do that. It must help the company decide what to throw the money at and what to cut."

Humanising Business

If I said we should humanise business, what would be your response?

"Humanising means merely dropping the mask of the brands, of the companies," said the Professor. "So humanising is something that is naturally tied to the exposition that we are facing nowadays.

"There is another metaphor that I use: In the past, when people used to go to a restaurant, they'd sit at the table and eat their food. The kitchen was hidden. Now the kitchen is in the middle of the restaurant. We see what the chefs are doing, how they are doing it, and where our food comes from, so that is a way to humanise the restaurant experience.

"Humanising means taking the mask away from ourselves and being real. The problem is that in the past, advertising helped a company to *create* a mask. With this mask, an opaque wall was built between the reality and the perception.

"Advertising in the past was about creating perceptions, and the perceptions may or may not have been the truth. Nowadays, you don't have the wall to hide behind. Advertisers are lost because too often the reality is not as beautiful as they are communicating. The communication no longer has value.

"The problem is not that marketing has changed; I believe that companies must change. Good marketing will just tell the truth. Marketing will change so that they are no longer lying or hiding their failures. They will tell the truth. They will be transparent.

"When you look at the whole company, traditional marketing has lost its importance because they are not creating or fabricating, anything. It's more important to be something that is real than to communicate something you are not."

The Question of Money

I asked the Professor to go back to his students and the question of why we are in business. It seems like the upper levels of management are obsessed with focusing on the financial part of their company and tend to forget why they got into business in the first place.

"You cannot forget that you need to make money, because that is the essence. I am not saying that all companies should turn into NGOs. But after all, if you think only of the money that you are making, you will be selling or providing a service to the *money* and not to the *people* who give you that money. The fact that people pay you is a compliment for something that you are serving them. And if you provide something that is either rationally or emotionally strong enough, they will give you money. They will pay you.

"Money is a *consequence* of good business. It's not the *essence* of it.

"If you only focus on the cost and the financial aspects of it, it's not sustainable in the long term. Of course, it may be easy to think that you have to achieve your goal this quarter, and then make a number of poor decisions in order to make that money quickly. But at what cost? It's not sustainable.

"On the other hand, if you understand your essence, and know that you are solving problems and providing good things or meeting your expectations, your business model is sustainable. Money is a consequence of this, and it's enjoyable. You're working because you see the value you're creating for people. You are creating emotion – it could be happiness, it could be any positive emotion – and then you create a positive cycle where you want to do better and you want to do more. Money is the consequence of this well-performed job".

I mentioned a clothing store in United States. Their sales were not going very well, and the sales manager decided to set up a sales competition to see who could sell the most. But it didn't motivate one of the employees. Instead of being the best *sales* person, she decided on her own to be the one who offered the best *service* and the best *customer experience.* For her it didn't matter how much time she spent helping and advising her customers. Her colleagues, on the other hand, didn't have time for that, because they were busy selling to as many people as possible. Who ended being the best performing salesperson? Of course it was the woman who decided to offer the best customer experience. Sometimes in our twisted minds we turn things upside down.

"This story illustrates that marketing will no longer be a *part* of the company," the Professor replied. "It will *be the company itself.* I don't believe we will see marketing departments within companies. The company will be the marketing because you can only communicate what you really are.

"Fusion needs to exist between business administration and marketing. How do you balance the financial results you need to achieve, and at the same time do things in a way that is expected by the audience or your 'guests,' as I like to call it. So the marketing won't only be communicating what you're doing; the marketing will be about *doing* positive things rather than merely *communicating* them. It will need a different mindset."

It was late, and the Professor needed to prepare for his next lecture. He bade me good-bye and I left his office to reflect on what we'd discussed.

From the taxi window on the superhighway I saw the results of the city planning that ceased to function back in the 1980s. To build a highway, the river that had once run through the main square of Vale do Anhangabaú had been directed into a concrete tunnel and, as in so many BRIC nations, rapid development had resulted in random urban sprawl.

I paid the taxi fare and started to walk to the city centre, also called the Central Zone of São Paulo. Many historical and important sights of town are in this area.

São Paulo's exploding traffic has driven people and businesses out of the city centre, leaving empty buildings, discount outlets, and parking lots. The main square sits above a highway and is bypassed by pedestrian flyovers, and there's nothing to invite people to come down to the square. It's run down, there's nowhere to sit and very little to enjoy.

Since 2008, the city administration and the local population have been working to revitalise the area that suffered degradation from the urban renewal. They're using the Danish architecture firm Gehl Architects, an urban research and design consultancy based in Copenhagen, Denmark.

Founded in 2000 by architect Helle Søholt and Professor Jan Gehl, the firm addresses global trends with a people-focused approach based on the human scale – the built environment's effect on activity patterns and interaction between people.

The lesson? It's not the façade of the building or the company that's important. Maybe in the past, the façade – or the advertising – could impress people. But not anymore. Transparency makes the façade an illusion.

It's the essence itself and how well it works for *people* that counts. It's something that's made by people for people. Buildings don't make a city. Advertising doesn't make a company.

Transparency makes you naked. A company and its marketing have to be indistinguishable.

Chapter 3

Frankenstein's Monster Looking for Love

After meeting the Professor, I was eager to meet the people behind the billboards – the movers and shakers of the advertising world. After reaching out to a journalist for contacts, the right person responded to my request for an interview. I soon found myself waiting in the reception area of São Paulo office of the most famous advertising agency of all time: Saatchi & Saatchi.

The environment was sleek, white, cool – like a Mondrian painting in three dimensions. It spoke of efficiency, purity of vision, and an absence of distraction. The only splash of colour was a big modernist painting covering one wall. The painting showed two people casually posed against a verdant background.

Being a leading global agency with one hundred and forty offices in seventy-six countries, Saatchi & Saatchi seemed the right place to look for new answers. If any, this agency represented the whole advertising industry, and I was excited to get into their heads, especially because much has happened since their heady days of the 1980s.

Founded in 1970 by brothers Maurice (now Lord Saatchi) and art collector Charles, Saatchi & Saatchi's early work included their campaign "Labour Isn't Working" on behalf of the Conservative Party before the 1979 UK general election and ongoing campaigns for British Airways. The agency was seen as producing breakthrough creative work with a bold attitude. The Saatchi brothers quickly expanded the company through business acquisitions. They wanted to become the largest advertising agency in the world. They succeeded, but the very same strategy also led to major turmoil for the agency

In 1997, Saatchi & Saatchi officially dropped the word "advertising" from its name, and their new global VRO Kevin Roberts instead turned Saatchi & Saatchi to an idea company and gave rise to the "lovemarks" philosophy. This met with scepticism in the advertising world – it seemed like what some people called the "advertising monster" was starting to fall in love.

Lovemarks

Lovemarks was a marketing concept intended to replace the idea of brands. The idea was first promoted in 2004 by Kevin Roberts, CEO of the agency, in his book of the same name. In the book Roberts asserted, "Brands are running out of juice." He considered that "love" was what was needed to rescue brands. Roberts asked, "What builds loyalty that goes beyond reason? What makes a truly great love stand out?"

According to Roberts, the following are the key ingredients to creating lovemarks:

Mystery – Great stories: past, present and future; taps into dreams, myths and icons, and inspiration.

Sensuality – Sound, sight, smell, touch, and taste.

Intimacy – Commitment, empathy, and passion.

Roberts explained that ordinary products are commodities that command neither love nor respect. Fads may attract love, but without respect this love is no more than temporary infatuation. Brands can attract lasting respect, but not necessarily love. Lovemarks command both respect and love. This is achieved through the trinity of mystery, sensuality, and intimacy.

For a brand to transcend to a lovemark, it has to create loyalty beyond reason which requires emotional connections that generate the highest levels of love and respect for the brand.

In the current world of marketing, there is a plethora of brands that use the concept of lovemarks behind their marketing strategies, such as The Coca-Cola Company, whose TV marketing campaigns are focused on transmitting emotions to the viewers of their advertisements.

Victor

I had not waited long in the cool white reception area before Victor, the strategic planning director for Saatchi & Saatchi, Brazil, came out and greeted me. He said he would rather talk outside, so we left his office and soon were strolling through the beautiful and immense Parque de Ibirapuera. Here in São Paulo's version of Central Park, visitors can wander the paths beside pleasant lagoons or rent a bicycle and cycle the pathways.

While we were walking, I engaged Victor in conversation. I asked him about the billboard ban in São Paulo.

"At this time, we really don't care about the ban," he replied matter-of-factly. "It's not an issue anymore. Sure, when it first happened it was a big hit. A lot of people were talking about it. But now even advertising marketers don't talk about it anymore.

"We have a business model that was implemented in the 1950s and it's been the same for the past sixty years. The work has changed a lot in terms of media consumption, technology, relationships, and what people desire for their life.

"If you compare the next generation like the Gen Y (also known as the Millennial Generation), it's completely different. For us, constructing lovemarks was necessary not because of competition but because people don't care anymore about brands. They just care about themselves.

"It's a kind of cliché, but the next generation want to be happy. Young people don't want to follow an idol. They have personal idols, such as a friend who has a band they love. This band will sell their music to just ten people, but those ten people love this band and they don't care about the famous singers like Bono from U2. These are *our* idols."

Victor laughed and made me remember that I wasn't in my twenties anymore. "Brands have less meaning for them because they don't follow idols," he said. "They don't follow philosophies. Their philosophy is their own philosophy, that's the point."

Defining Meaning

I said to Victor that "meaning" is quite an interesting word in this context. The 'meaning quotient' coined by McKinsey looks at how we (especially the new generation) are hunting for meaning. It's like we're starving for it. It seems like we have hit the roof of Maslow's hierarchy of needs. How can companies help us find meaning?

"We have to put meanings into brands," said Victor, "because, for instance, Coca-Cola doesn't sell soft drinks. They sell *happiness*. Virgin doesn't sell flight tickets. They sell *freedom*. These deeper meanings go beyond language or culture. They work globally.

"For example, let's say that Samsung is the first company to have a certain kind of television. I walk through the electronics fair and I go to the LG stand and there's a big display saying they too are the first one to have this kind of television. But that's not the fight. The fight is about *meaning*. Why I would buy a Samsung instead of LG? It's the same technology, probably made in the same factory. If you don't have meaning for people, and if you don't have values that people can recognise, you won't have a chance.

"Value is a meaning. A classic example is Microsoft versus Apple, where you could say Microsoft is a great brand while Apple is a lovemark. It has something more. It's kind of like a movement.

"Apple doesn't sell products. They challenge the status quo. That's what Apple is about. And by the way, they sell computers."

But is Apple really still fighting the status quo? From being the underdog with a four per cent market share to capturing twenty-five per cent of the computer and tablet market, and now without its charismatic leader who embodied all their values, we might see a company that needs to reinvent itself. Values are not just a label you put on your product; they're something organic you need to nurture all the time in a volatile world.

Our walk eventually led us to the restaurant at Sao Paulo's Modern Art Museum (MAM), located like a gem in the middle of the park. The museum was founded in 1948 as an initiative of Francisco Matarazzo Sobrinho and his wife, famed aristocrat and art patron Yolanda Penteado. Established in Ibirapuera Park, its development was inspired by the Museum of Modern Art (MoMA) in New York, and was one of the first establishments dedicated to modern art in Brazil.

Over lunch, we continued our discussion.

"Take this restaurant, for example," said Victor. "Maybe the meaning is not to change the world but to serve the best food they know how to cook, for the best price they can offer, and make people have a great moment while they are eating."

It's simple, yet there are so many restaurants where you're left with a bad experience, like the people there don't care about you. You can taste it when people have prepared the food with love.

Human Values

"You have to find a human value that can be expressed in an ad in different countries," continued Victor, "and that's hard. It's really hard because you can make a list of several brands that have the same values and the same target market. So how can you make one more gratifying than the other? You have the same value and you have the same meaning in people's lives.

"It's hard, it's really hard, and this is the challenge facing many brands. I worked for a huge brand here. It's the biggest beer brand in Brazil…"

While he was talking I became surprised at how much Victor was still talking about ads and brands despite the fact that Saatchi & Saatchi wanted to be known as an idea agency that created lovemarks, not an advertising agency working for brands. But at the same time he was also talking about values and meaning. I sensed he wanted to solve today's problems using yesterday's solutions.

"Take Guaraná Antarctica," he said. "It's a very Brazilian brand. You can list three Brazilian brands that people would recognise worldwide, or Brazilians recognise as a real Brazilian brand, and this is one of them. But this is an attribute, not a value. Being Brazilian is an attribute; being natural is an attribute. Being from the Amazon rainforest, and using the fruit of guaraná from the Amazon forest, is an attribute.

"The problem is that there's a lack of meaning for this brand. People drink it, but when they choose between Coca-Cola and Guaraná Antarctica in terms of brand, not in terms of the soft drink itself, they would rather choose Coca-Cola instead of Guaraná. This is because Coca-Cola has a lot of meaning. That's why Coca-Cola has fifty per cent of the market and Guaraná has ten per cent.

"It's not about the company, because you can have the same logistics and the same great employees. Guaraná Antarctica cannot overcome the meaning of Coca-Cola. Guaraná Antarctica can have good prices, good logistics, and a good business-to-business relationship, but in the end the supermarkets would rather sell Coca-Cola than Guaraná. Not because people prefer the beverage itself, but because people prefer the brand.

"I can say all that because I've worked for this brand for four years, so I know what I'm talking about. Guaraná's message is, 'We are natural, we are refreshing, we are for young people, and we are from the Amazon.' Meanwhile, Coca-Cola says one word: 'happiness.' That's stronger than being natural. Would you rather have a natural life or a happy life?"

It was a very good point and not just valid if you sold soft drinks. Like the Professor had pointed out, emotions are also valid for a business selling to other businesses. Then why can't Guaraná become the leading brand?

"If I promise happiness," said Victor, "I will only succeed in reinforcing what Coca-Cola says. It will be hard beating Coca-Cola using the same language that it uses."

So you kind of have to figure out something that's even better than Coca-Cola?

"Yes. This is what Pepsi does. They talk about being the next generation."

I thought that was very interesting. What about Mc-Donald's, because they have also promoted themselves as the happy restaurant? You can have a Happy Meal, just like Coca-Cola sells happiness. I don't know about Brazil, but especially in Denmark, and also in the US, consumers have new values. They want to be healthy, and everyone knows that McDonald's is unhealthy food.

"The same in Brazil," said Victor. "Not the same level, but because of that they are offering different meals right now. For instance, in Brazil they have a very popular dish with rice and beans and beef, chicken, or salmon. It's very popular. And they sell that at McDonald's. This is not fast food; this is real food, home food. They are trying to reinvent the business. Their signs used to read, 'McDonald's Hamburgers.' Now they just have 'McDonald's' because they still sell hamburgers, French fries, and all those chicken-somethings."

Could it be, I asked, because of the high level of education, the transparency, it's getting increasingly difficult to sell junk food? Because now we can suddenly say, "Hey, it's a bad product."

"I have two kids," said Victor. "They have never drunk soft drinks. We have never gone to McDonald's because I don't think it's healthy for them. I chose to do this at the very beginning of their lives because it will give them a chance when they're young to have healthy lives. It doesn't mean that my kids will never drink soft drinks or eat hamburgers. It means that it will be easier to resist even when all their friends are eating French fries and Big Macs. That type of food will seem strange to them, and it won't taste very good."

"I think education is the key. Ignorance makes it easier to manipulate people."

Is This Really Something New?

Victor was a very sympathetic guy, but as he continued talking, I really couldn't see the connection between the work done by Victor and his team in São Paulo and the fact that Saatchi's CEO Kevin Roberts was claiming that marketing was dead. That Saatchi & Saatchi had transformed from an "advertising" agency to an "idea" agency sounded compelling, but it could well be an "Emperor's New Clothes" or old wine in a new bottle.

Maybe it was hype from the advertising industry.

Their "ideas" for the beer brand Skol "Gringo Your Selfie" campaign consisted of letting Brazilians take selfies with tourists.

For the instant noodle producer Nissin, they proposed a scheme to cook instant noodles in outer space.

An unmanned rocket took a capsule that was built to carry the ingredients for the recipe created by French chef Emmanuel Bassoleil to an altitude of more than one hundred kilometres and then ejected it into space. The idea was for the noodles to reach boiling point when the capsule passed through the mesosphere on its way back to earth. (The mesosphere is the layer of Earth's atmosphere that is responsible for, among other things, burning up meteors and now also for preparing space noodles!)

The rocket was launched in time to kick off the celebration for the fiftieth anniversary of Nissin Miojo Lámen in Brazil.

Shooting a space rocket to the mesosphere to cook noodles in the name of changing the history of cuisine forever might sound innovative – but it could also sound like a cheap new gimmick to get peoples' attention without any real substance.

Some of the advertising industry's biggest initiatives – from Edward Bernays's "torches of freedom" to Saatchi & Saatchi's endless advertising campaigns – confirm what the Canadian neurologist Donald B. Calne said:

"The essential difference between emotion and reason is that emotion leads to action while reason leads to conclusions."

Lots of companies still have to learn that fact. But too often the emotional appeals have no substance, no values, and end up being just another way to interrupt via the mass media.

The Saatchi & Saatchi that used to shake up the old establishment in the conservative United Kingdom seems to have become the fat cat itself. But Saatchi & Saatchi is just one of the many traditional advertising agencies that needs to re-invent themselves. Lots of them are bleeding or closing down because times have changed. Some of them have tried to succeed in the digital world, only to have created a lot of noise there. Their Facebook ads are often just physical billboards turned digital.

Leaving Victor in the peaceful surroundings of the city park, I re-entered the chaotic city. Maybe the green park made the city look prettier, but it was overpowered by the rest of the city that was all concrete and pollution. Maybe it was the nature of the advertising industry, that it could only put on a mask on its clients but fundamentally not change anything. The ad men wanted to make their clients the biggest but not the best in the market. That is a fundamental difference in your business strategy.

I started to walk through the streets, wondering where to go. I felt I had reached a dead end in São Paulo's labyrinth. After speaking with the Professor and the Agency, it was time to find a company.

Chapter 4

The Key to This Business is Personal Relationships

I was sceptical from the start. Though the billboard ban in São Paulo was an interesting experiment, I still had my doubts whether I could find companies the rest of the world could learn from.

A journalist contact insisted that I go to a suburb of São Paulo called Alphaville to visit a company there. It sounded like a name you would give a space colony on Mars. Perhaps it was fitting; after all, Brazil, unlike Europe, has almost no past, only future. That makes it impossible to look backwards to find solutions, which often are too outdated anyway for tomorrow's challenges.

The positive side is that being cut off from the past can spark innovation.

Even the capital of Brazil is just fifty years old. It's a city built from scratch. Brasilia is not only a planned city, it is a planned capital. In 1960 Brasília replaced Rio de Janeiro as Brazil's centre of government. Just five years before, the area resembled a desert, with no people, scarce water, and few animals and plants.

By the close of the twentieth century, Brasília held the distinction of being the largest city in the world that had not existed at the beginning of the century.

Alphaville

I was headed for a similarly planned city, though much smaller than Brasilia. Alphaville was created by a construction company in the 1970s. The impetus was that the São Paulo megalopolis was beginning to show increasing crime rates, traffic jams, and other forms of urban problems, and consequently suburban developments gained popularity, both for modern industrial and commercial ventures and for the wealthy and upper-middle-class residents of the city.

Today, the original Alphaville site has thirty-three gated areas, with more than 20,000 residences. The business area is already a small city, withover two thousand businesses, including eleven schools and universities, with a daily movement of more than 150,000 people.

My first thoughts about Alphaville were of the film of the same name. *Alphaville: une étrange aventure de Lemmy Caution (Alphaville: A Strange Adventure of Lemmy Caution)* is a 1965 black-and-white French science fiction film noir directed by Jean-Luc Godard I had seen a couple of years earlier. Combining the genres of dystopian science fiction and film noir, the film was shot on location in Paris with the night-time streets of the capital becoming the streets of Alphaville, while modernist glass and concrete buildings (that in 1965 were new and strange architectural designs) represented the city's interiors.

The film is about a society where people who show signs of emotion are gathered up, interrogated, and executed. It evokes the corporate culture you find in many companies. It's all about profit. When you speak to the people there – expecting to get service – it's like talking to computers. The concept of the individual self, the personal relationship, has been crushed under the profit-optimised machine of a company.

Eloi and Flytour

The company I visited in the real Alphaville is called Flytour, which operates as a travel agency for both companies and individuals. Their 2,300 employees arrange business trips for big companies like IBM and Microsoft.

While Flytour is a corporation, the campus struck me as very uncorporate. I felt like I was in a theme park rather than an office complex. This place was really built for people by people. After having visited countless offices, that at the best have been built by good architects but at the worst looked more like bland boxes, here I felt like I was at home.

I was offered a coffee in their canteen, where I was amazed to see a life-sized replica shark like the one in *Jaws* that looked as if it were crashing through the ceiling. "Why?" I asked the PR team accompanying me.

"It's a metaphor for our competitors," they said. "We're doing very well, and when we enjoy the good food in our canteen that's beautifully decorated, it's easy to forget that we are not swimming in the ocean of opportunities alone. There are competitors and you have to be ready for them."

What a great way to prevent complacency, I thought. You can either say it or show it. And I'm sure the shark is vividly remembered by everyone who enters the canteen.

The next thing that hit me was a pool with a fountain and a statue in Greek style surrounded by a beautiful green lawn.

They've even built their own lighthouse, which towers above two of the palm-shaded buildings. Having been tipped off by the PR guys that this is no random choice, I reflected upon it as a symbol of a company that is standing up tall, guiding the way, making sure people stay clear of obstacles up ahead. *There is no need to fear*, it says. This is a company headquarters that keeps telling stories wherever I look.

I met Eloi, their marketing manager. He's also the son of the founder, who has the same name, only pronounced slightly differently. Maybe Eloi's father really wanted to see his progeny continue long after his earthly demise.

Eloi surprised me by starting our conversation by showing me a colourful cartoon drawing of their founder sitting in a small boat, fishing. His fishing line traced a sweeping S-curve in the bright blue sky, and formed a time line. The time line started in 1974 and extended to the last stop of *Futuro: 2014 a 2018.* On the far left of the picture, a rocky outcropping was topped by the company lighthouse.

The scene represented the whole company. The placid ocean symbolised opportunities. The man in the boat gives direction. You always have a point to go to and a map. All employees aim for the same philosophy on the same boat. It works very well.

He also showed me a graphic poster featuring the Brazilian flag and geometric shapes. The text below the graphic read: "This chart represents the history of our Group. The flag represents one hundred per cent of our patriotism. The largest ellipse means the beginning of a dream, a solid company. The smaller ones mean the continuing evolution of this achievement. The fish represent our achievements. The birds show unity and the spirit of peace in our relationships."

I asked Eloi if all of their 2,300 employees knew about this.

"All of them," replied Eloi. "Everybody attends immersion classes. We have five classrooms. We award diplomas to five thousand people a year. Everything about our philosophy and our history is taught.

"It's our DNA. We're a corporation, but we don't see it as a corporation. We work with the understanding that the main value of the company is our people, and they need to be engaged with the philosophy, the DNA, and the history of the company. That's how we create our culture."

I was impressed. I had never seen a company with such strong storytelling. How often have business leaders stood up in front of their employees showing graphs, numbers, and endless PowerPoint slides? For so long it has puzzled me how companies that from the outside seem to do all the right things but only because they bought all the fancy programs and systems sold by consultants using a lot of buzzwords. It's not a system that's needed; it's spirit!

I told Eloi that I noticed LEGO bricks symbolising the year the company started.

"Yes," he replied. "I love LEGO too. I used to play with it when I was a kid. In our house we have big walls with large shelves for LEGO models.

"I like the history because LEGO is a family company. We're also a family company. We've learned a lot from them."

I recalled an article I had read a few months earlier about LEGO. Unlike public companies, they are not forced to look short-term to satisfy their shareholders. Family businesses can stick to their values. There is nothing wrong in earning money, but without a purpose and values, it makes it more difficult for people to dedicate themselves to creating something great.

Business is Personal

"The key to this business is personal relationships," said Eloi. "Our customers trust us. Let's say someone gets married, and they're wondering where to go on their honeymoon. I'll say, 'Go to this hotel. Stay three days here, another four days there. Rent this car. Eat this food. Go to this restaurant.' It's people to people."

"Too much business and customer service is going online. But software cannot interact with you. When you have a problem – say, you can't get a flight – whom do you call? You need real humans."

"I can tell you it works. Ninety-five per cent of our clients are returning clients. The relationships are strong and they have confidence in us. We're always adapting to the client and making sure that everybody is important. We won't let anybody stay in the airport. If you have a problem, if you got in late, we're going to find another flight for you. We have to make it work. We never know who missed the flight. Was it the CEO or the sales guy? We treat everyone equally."

"It's not the brand that sells. It's word of mouth. For example, if you're a businessman, you're looking for the same service – which is flying – and having all expenses covered by the company. Let's say you do your travel planning with another company, and your friend says to you, 'I prefer to go by Flytour.' Really? Why? And that's how the conversation starts. Most of our clients come from recommendations from their colleagues."

I tried to push Eloi to see if that were really true. Was all of it repeat customers and word of mouth? Eloi told me they really didn't do any marketing for their B2B segment, but for their B2C segment they do use traditional advertising. One also has to understand, he said, that Brazil is a country where lots of people can't even read.

"In this business," he said, "What wins is not the ad. It's not the marketing brand. If you only look at the price and you look at an image like in an ad, it's very hard to measure what you're buying. It's like if you go into a car dealer intending to buy the cheapest car. When you get there and you see the differences between the various models of cars, all at the same dealership, then you say, 'I want this one. I don't want that anymore.' You see the difference."

Don't Sell on Price Alone

"I don't believe in selling on the basis of price," continued Eloi. "If you only focus on the price, you don't create a relationship with the customer. You've sold yourself for short-term money.

"There might be competitors that are cheaper, but people also worry about the quality. Is this a good place to buy because it's cheaper? Will I regret it if I buy it here? We have these kinds of thoughts about quality. You get what you pay for. Good quality and service have their price."

It was like he was repeating a statistic published by the Rockefeller Institute / Tarp Studies about why customers leave a company in favour of another one. Surprisingly, for only nine per cent it was because of the price. For sixty-eight per cent it was the lack of dialogue and communication.

"We made an interesting video two years back," said Eloi. "Before I came here, my brother was responsible for marketing. What are the challenges when a person has a life of travel? When you're at home, life has a regular rhythm, but then you have to travel for business. It's hard. You have to leave the kids at home. You have to catch a flight. You have to worry about whether the meeting is going to go well. The video shows how well you are treated while travelling, so you don't have to worry about that. At least you can focus on what is really important to you, which is family and creating a good business. Flytour takes good care of you when you are travelling so you can take care of what is important for you. It's a strong emotion, and that is very valid in the business world.

"We also have a software app providing you with maps and information about your destination. If you're going to a destination like the Hotel Meliá, for example, and you enter 'destination,' it shows which direction the hotel is. It's a great service. It's all about coming up with new and smarter ways to service your customers and make their lives better.

"If I provide great service, people will talk about it. I don't have to do advertising in media. They will sell it for me. The customer will say, 'Oh, you see I bought the product here and I received great service,' and then you'll check it out yourself because the people that you trust are giving you the advice.

"It's the best marketing in businesses that exists. It's about relationships. I will say the future is about relationships. With a good relationship it's also a lot easier to cross-sell, up-sell, and after-sell. But the cross-sell, up-sell, and after-sell must be seen as a service."

I love when companies can redefine their sales and marketing. Why not make your service your marketing.

"We ask, 'How was your flight? Was everything okay? How was your vacation? Next year, where would you like to go?'

"We give advice. Our people work after the sale. It's really what happens *after* the sale that's important, not the first sale you did. But for a lot of companies will sell something to you, and then suddenly they don't care about you anymore. 'I already sold that stuff to you,' they'll say. 'I don't need to take care of you. You already bought it.'"

I remarked that this attitude often comes from ineffective incentive programmes inside the company. If your sales people get a bonus each time they get a new customer, that's where the focus will be. And they won't care about your old customers. We need to see our business as relationship-based and not transaction-based. After the acquisition cost of getting a new customer, you often need the customer for two or three years before they're profitable.

"Don't sell people a product," continued Eloi. "Serve them. Start listening to them. You have to sit and talk to them and see what they're really looking at. Then you can help them in the best way. But for that you need educated employees. What if I had an employee who never caught a plane? How can they sell or serve a customer who is going to fly? Your employees don't know what you're talking about but they have to sell it. How can you do that? How can they talk about a product if they haven't had it?

"We understand that when you teach an employee to talk about a product or a country or a destination, they get really happy.

"Most of our knowledge about tourism is from university. We have four to five years of courses. All new employees have to go for a one-month introduction, and then you have to go to specialised training in our business in some area. In our company, you can end up having a bachelor's degree, and it's a very respectable degree."

Investing in Employees

I suggested that for Flytour to offer employees a business degree or a degree at university was a cutting edge idea. For most, being a company representative on the phone is a position of low status. Top management may even see such employees as an expense rather than an investment in customer care and relationship building.

As we walked around we passed by a football that had been placed on the floor in the middle of the office. It rested on a green mat that looked like a miniature pitch.

On the football, employees had written their goals for the year. Like football players need to score goals, the employees have goals too. What a perfect metaphor for a country of football fanatics!

We then moved on to a big TV screen showing a dashboard.

"I want to show you something very interesting," said Eloi. "Here we show all our daily numbers, our goals and results. You might assume this feel-good company is all about soft values, but it's also a very data-driven company. Setting goals is integrated in the company culture too. Our goals are all 'live' for everyone to see. We're transparent for all our employees."

I was then introduced to Eloi's brother Chris. He's the business director for the business travel division.

"It's in our balanced scorecard (BSC)," said Chris after I asked him how they measure their customer satisfaction. "Our goal is ninety-two per cent happy clients. We have several tools that measure that on a daily basis, like the call experience. That has a value on the balanced scorecard, so twenty points of the balanced scorecard is related to client satisfaction.

"That represents twenty per cent of the salary also, so we use the BSC to pay two extra salaries a year for all the employees. Also it's sales, revenue, training, client satisfaction, and growth of productivity. The goal for productivity is forty per cent of the total value, and then ten per cent growth of sales and revenue, then twenty. The total is one hundred per cent, so every six months we shut down the balanced scorecard and see all the measurements and what were the achievements, and they get an extra salary paid."

It was time to leave, and before I said goodbye he handed me a copy of their company brochure. The first two pages had nothing to do about their services. Instead it showed pictures of their employees, and also a woman with the title 'cleaner.' This was really a people's company.

The taxi drove me out of Alphaville. Going back to the city centre felt like being in a time machine travelling from the future back to the present. If more companies were managed in the same way, I'm sure we would have many more happy employees. And that is really the key for a great company. It's difficult to create happy customers and give them great experiences when they are served by unhappy employees.

The company really showed that something as old-fashioned as personal relations and great customer service really counts. Companies that will not evolve and put people first will die, because the best people don't want to work there.

It's also an example of a company that is investing in its people. In order to give the best possible customer experience, their employees need to be educated.

Luckily, they are not alone. As I return to the city centre I see bikes. But they are not like any other bike, they are part of a movement, and one daring company has redefined marketing – forever.

Chapter 5

#thischangestheworld

I wanted to find a company that used to advertise through the city's billboards and the traditional mass marketing channels, but because of the constraints put on them by São Paulo's Clean City law had to find new and better ways. And what if that company was the one you least expected to innovate in an industry that during the financial crises had gained a reputation of men in suits only thinking of money?

A bank! Yes, if a bank could lead the way, anybody should be able to do it.

When pondering banks and their marketing schemes, I thought of this cautionary tale. In February 2012, Danske Bank, one of the biggest banks in Europe, decided to revamp its image. The bank commissioned an expensive TV commercial entitled "A New Normal Demands New Standards." The Hollywood-quality ad featured grim scenes of police repression and faceless workers that seemed to be taken straight from George Orwell's *1984*. For most viewers the effect was deeply disturbing and upsetting. All the things that were supposedly considered "the new normal" evoked the creepy New World Order agenda, whether it be a police state, the repression of free speech, or brainwashing children. The message was *supposed* to be that the bank recognised and understood the reality of today's world. The ad backfired and became a target of derision.

It was a façade and times had changed. People could see through it and the ad was a huge fiasco.

What if the advertising was not just fancy words and slick images? What if marketing could actually materialise something of real value for people? Not *pretend* to be something, but actually *be* it?

Itaú Unibanco and Bike Sampa

With headquarters in São Paulo, Brazil, Itaú Unibanco is the largest financial conglomerate in the southern hemisphere and is the tenth largest bank in the world by market value. Their strategy is shaped by their vision, which is to be the leading bank in sustainable performance and customer satisfaction.

One day, Itaú executives had a meeting with an American named Peter Cabral, who is the business executive/director of Samba Transportes Sustentáveis in São Paulo. Soon the bank's marketing budget was no longer invested in billboards. It was becoming a movement.

Here in São Paulo, Peter had convinced the largest bank in Latin America to spend their marketing money on sponsoring Bike Sampa – a fleet of rental bikes available to the public at a bike stations throughout the city. It's an ambitious project; the goal is to have three thousand bicycles available at three hundred solar-powered and wireless-linked stations. To use the shared system, you simply register online at movesamba.com.br.

In a 2012 press release, Cicero Araujo, the bank's director of institutional relations and governments, said, "Itaú Unibanco adopted the platform of urban mobility because the bank believes in the use of bicycles as a viable means of transportation in traffic within the big cities. The excellent utilisation numbers prove the success of the programme. This endearing acceptance of the bicycles is a source of pride for us and, as Bike Sampa is still expanding, we believe that the bike will integrate more and more to the city every day and will be an alternative for travelling short distances."

I met Peter in a symbol of American counter-culture business success – a local Starbucks. As I entered I recalled that as Starbucks grew from a few coffee shops to a global empire, the company did no advertising. None. Zero. Its phenomenal expansion was accomplished purely by word of mouth.

Connections between people and their city.

Coffees in hand, we sat down. Peter looks a bit like Abraham Lincoln – tall and authoritative. I asked him to give me some insight into the philosophy behind Bike Sampa.

"It's about creating a movement or phenomenon that is moving very fast, almost faster than the formation of habit," replied Peter. "Society as a whole, holistically, needs to develop an affinity and a curiosity to realise whether or not the bike – the dual-wheeled human locomotive frame – can fit into their modus operandi, their daily life. When people hear about it, they are curious.

They will come to you in the morning and they will look at the rental bike station and say, 'Well, look, my friend told me about it.' They see something on the web – on Facebook or Instagram – or a friend says something or posts something, and then there is some form of institutionalised campaign where the mayor publishes something about the bicycle that is wonderful.

"With bikes we are creating lifelines. We are creating a line of visual communication and a platform whereby drivers of motorised vehicles have to share the public space with other types of vehicles – this time a non-motorised type of vehicle. They start to understand that it is not only a concept, but a movement.

"It grows organically. When you work with a product, a system, or in this case a service that relies on folks and individuals, and that appeals to one's collective sense of sharing, that's primordial or primitive. We are gregarious, social animals.

"Each one of us can take a step back and realise that this rented bike is something I can use to go to school. This is something I can use once I get off at a subway station, and it's mine, it's Christian's, and it's also John's.

I can hop on it and cycle one or two kilometres, one or two clicks, deliver it, and get rid of it at another station. Then Christian comes along and he's going to get on at another bike point and utilise the same bike that I just dropped off, and will ride it all the way home because he has a bike point right next to his apartment building.

"You had five hundred people doing this at first. Soon ten thousand bike users connected with another twenty thousand bike users, and all of a sudden you understand that this is not just doing A to B, B to C. This is organic, it's viral, and it works at a macro level.

"You understand the possibilities of sharing, and you still have a strong individual sense of presence. Then you realise that, holistically, this is a movement. It appeals to a social level and it's a more sophisticated way of relating to society, and that sharing leads to something greater. When you start to share resources, you begin to wonder whether this should have been the way it was done all along. This may sound a bit extremist, but you can build a world like that."

Radical Thinking

Peter had looked at marketing on a complete different level. That was radical thinking, and I could easily imagine people accuse him of being a dreamer. It brought to mind the saying that the people who are crazy enough to think they can change the world are the ones who do. "You have to think big," I said.

"Yes, you have to think big," said Peter. "The reality of São Paulo today makes you wonder about it, because at an incipient stage you have a system that (as opposed to other cities and their systems) was in the beginning very naïve and very reticent regarding its culture. The history of São Paulo in relation to its size and proportions and demographics is very low-key. We came in, made it work, and now you see bikes in the most unusual places.

"Perhaps this is not unusual to you. You come from abroad, and you know where those things belong in your average urban landscape.

"But imagine someone emerging from under a rock and seeing bicycles and little bike pictograms and signs saying you're too close to the kerb, make some room, signals communicating with drivers that tell them that the traffic has been reduced so that people can share a public resource. Individual people, on motorised and non-motorised vehicles, can co-exist in this area. Such a person will understand that this is a movement. It's organic and it changes the way the city relates to people and the way that people experience the city. It's sweet mobility. Your mobility context changes; you are no longer enveloped or separated from the city. You feel the city at a different level. You see and hear and smell and feel the cold, the warmth, the wind.

The Impact of Bike Sampa

I really liked the idea of how marketing can actually serve people. What was the impact?

"We have accomplished all of this in a short time span," said Peter. "In just three years since the launch of Bike Sampa, the experience is surprisingly positive. We have folks who use and popularise it and want more. When you put our bicycling programme in perspective and you go back forty or fifty years, or twenty, thirty years in France, Denmark, or even Norway, you understand that you had a lot of work back then developing a mindset, a predisposition, and a lot of work in educating.

"It's a phenomenon that took time to build. So considering and analysing the European bicycle experience in comparison to the Brazilian bicycle experience, I believe the movement has accomplished a lot in a short space of time."

I agreed that was true, because it took a long time in Denmark (where I am from) to create that culture. I asked Peter about where he thought this movement was in its life cycle or bell curve as described in *The law of diffusion of innovation*. Had it peaked? Was it sustainable over years or even decades?

"That's interesting," he replied, "because I think about that every day. I think about it in terms of marketing and as a business proposition. What is the next market step? What do I have to do today to continue to be competitive and have the best possible technical solutions? How do I cater to this market? How do I go outside of this market and tell our story? Can we share our story in a regional market?

"I believe it's our obligation to share this Brazilian experience. If we have tropicalised something from Europe, I feel I have the obligation to go to Santiago, to go to Bogota, to go further north, or to go to Buenos Aires. We did in fact win the contract for public tendering there, so we'll be opening there soon. Next time you go to Buenos Aires you'll see our system there, too.

"I often think about what we need to do to have good technology, services, a business model that will allow for a sustainable business, and public-private partnerships that are good. Which market do we have? Where can we tell our story? We want to master that story."

I felt mesmerised when he was talking. This was a guy who was unlike many sales and marketing people who just want to hit their sales goals and get next month's pay cheque. Peter was talking with passion. He was there for something bigger.

"There is a role for the bicycle. Bike Sampa raised that flag and was provocative. There is a perception that what works now must grow to the point where you have more options. To grow you need sustainable business models."

Legacy

I asked Peter how he came up with the idea of a movement.

"You need to feel a certain level of responsibility," he said. "We understand that we're living in a historical moment. The bicycle could make the difference. The bicycle has a legacy and potential. We need companies with a vision and the ability to say, 'We will take that first step.' From a position of social responsibility as a company and their shareholders, their mission and values drive the effort.

"To take that first step you need vision and character, and you need a strong belief that what you have today will have a legacy and is worth doing. Itaú Bank has that. They took that vision and took the service and used its values to tell a story."

I was impressed by Itaú Bank's bold move. It's not about advertising any more. It's not about propaganda; it's about legacy that is so beyond traditional marketing that I am sure it would be difficult to grasp for most sales and marketing departments.

"Itaú Bank saw an opportunity and decided to tell their story in such a way as to create a positive impact," said Peter. "They built a platform, and that platform appeals to social responsibility and social integration, and appeals to society in general in a fashion where they understand the direct benefit. They don't see that as a traditional branding campaign but as a company that took a step, raised the flag, and set the pace on something that simply had to be done. They see a municipal entity engaged, building infrastructure, preoccupied with education (traffic education) and campaigns, and they slowly see a society that is more forgiving and that is starting to understand models and means of transportation. They understand other solutions to the problem of transport. It was never about publicity but about building a legacy.

"Within the bank, the project owner is not marketing, not propaganda, not visual. It is not a marketing programme. We don't have marketing media, capital, or finance. It's completely different."

I was curious to know whether he believed this project could also be a showcase for other businesses. How could

Peter see this being applied in other cases? Is that the future of marketing?

"I think it's the future," said Peter. "It's about creating a legacy and a movement that understands the benefits of such a service or product. It could be infrastructure or a service, public works or education, in any sector. The dogma, private or public, in the sense that we see it in black and white, and we see that the only way one sector can come together with another is contractual – I am the public sector and I need something, so I tender, you supply. That works, but there are more innovative ways to shape that and make that something bigger and greater and more sophisticated, which is in line with today's needs, challenges, economy, societal needs, societal growth, micro-economy, and macro-economy.

"That opens up a new ecosystem, and it jump starts and motivates companies to assume and understand that they are part of something bigger. Public and private are both part of something bigger.

"Once they are part of something bigger, they start to think collectively. All of a sudden, social responsibility and social entrepreneurship are providing them with a better mission and values. That is the change. That change can happen business-wise. They can grow."

From Marketing to Movement

I asked Peter how could the movement ensure that people become customers in the end? Companies might be very sceptical spending money on a movement when the results might seem elusive.

"Think of a business and an advertising interface where X amount goes to advertising. Maybe just skip the interface and you are right in front of the market. You realise the market has been there all along. You just have to be more organic and less artificial. Once you are closer to the market, you become it and you develop a sense of a legacy. There are creative ways to build sustainable business models to provide a basic service or a super product that represent a new way of doing things.

"Think about this: If a company has a million dollars to spend on advertising, all of a sudden they might say, 'Let's clean the river.' The chief marketing officers would immediately ask, 'How can we show our customers that we have been cleaning the river? We need to have a billboard here and put our brand here. We'll have a little dragon boat, and we will activate our brand on the boat. We will do this and that. We'll have a uniform and go on print.' It's all about that.

"We say that you don't have to do that. Take our bikes. The thematics, the visual communication, is elusive and conducive to brand evaluation. Why don't you tell a story? Why don't you tell the story that you cleaned the river? How can you appeal to a five- or twelve-year-old kid? How do you appeal to a mother who is pregnant and is about to deliver and she's worried about pollution? How do you appeal at a grass roots level? How do you start a movement to express or manifest that in a contagious fashion?

"We live in a world where people push information and download information. I'm always connected and I'm thinking you're the same. We are animals of today's living. Two or three generations into the future may be ultra- or hyper-connected.

"People want to socialise and share experiences. We need to find a creative way to tell that story. To editorialise it.

"Find a way to make it organic," he told me. "People get in touch through social networks. We are close to one million users of the bike app.

"I have very interesting experiences, riding along, talking to folk. People tell me, 'I never thought I could bring my kids downtown and relax. I used to come here with my mother and father; but nowadays I take my children on play dates from school to a friend's house.'"

I recalled my own childhood and suddenly understood how powerful stories can be. They can be very emotional, and you get a natural urge to share those stories.

I liked what Peter was saying. He sounded like an American optimist, so I decided to play the part of a European pessimist. I was going to poke him a little.

"We all know there are bad marketers out there," I said. "Companies without the right values. They want to have a social profile, a façade, but what is behind the façade can be difficult for the rest of us to see. How can we see through that?"

"That's human nature," he said. "That's the lack of balance and collective understanding, of belonging and identity. It's a serious challenge to see through that. I think that for the sake of the market, the consumer needs to be better educated and have access to more information, because if they have access to information they will raise their standards. By raising their standards, the markets will adapt to that new standard. How do we see through it? Get closer, share more information, use the access we have to today, make things organic – these are all reasons to get closer.

"One more reason to share experiences: you can have that façade, and you see it every day. But it doesn't last forever. As a whole, society and the market has a tendency to get more straightforward, sensible, socially responsible, and humanised. The collective perspective with a backbone of social responsibility is the only way for sustained market growth based on the consumer as a human being."

I told Peter I shared that vision. We live in a world that is becoming more transparent. It is difficult for companies to hide and keep up that façade.

"By being opaque, they lose more," he agreed. "They lose more shareholders. These days you have shareholders, product investors, funds, that make a point to have in their portfolio either private or equity companies that have some sort of social engagement or responsibility.

"Find an innovative way to tell that story. Make a legacy. The first question I ask any time I look at an investment, every marketing plan, every piece of communication, is, 'What's the legacy? How much content? What is the context – Is it organic? Is it not? Is it sustainable? Or not? What is its impact? Is it positive?'"

I asked Peter what his dream was for ten years from now.

"Ten years is too soon," he said. "I'm looking further out. I see a need for people to get close to one another, to share resources and information and the planet. Everything is inviting us to share. Our resources are everything: where we live, our tools. Soon we will have a new generation who realise we are too big and too individualistic, that there are too many of us, and it's going to be difficult to share at the end. Otherwise we will reach a point where it is not possible – resource-wise, economy-wise, market-wise, business-wise. The kids today understand we need to create that mindset for our own sake. I am talking anthropologically, sociologically. I'm talking about the marketplace, and we need to consider that, because there is a trend: Is it sustainable? Is it aligned with our trajectory?

"More human, less machine dependent, more movement-wise. Machines, mechanics – we can all do that. The thought process, the mindset has to change. We need a Shangri-La – an earthly paradise – like in James Hilton's *Lost Horizon*, and companies can provide that."

Peter doesn't only have a vision that's great to tell; it's contagious, so much that it surpasses any traditional marketing campaign. Itaú Bank has the numbers to prove the effectiveness of the campaign. Itaú wants to be not just the place where you put your money for safekeeping; it wants to change peoples' lives. In order to spread the word about its initiatives, including Bike Sampa, the bank launched #thischangestheworld. The bank reports that one-quarter of all searches related to the brand are #thischangestheworld, and both customers and non-customers are increasingly identifying Itaú not just with financial responsibility, which you would expect from a bank, but as a force for social good.

I sipped the last of my coffee and said goodbye to Peter. Later I tried one of the Bike Sampa rental bikes, and found myself zooming through the streets, dodging pedestrians and feeling the vibrations of the handlebars and the wind in my hair. Suddenly I realised that just as Peter had said, I was now part of the story. The message had become the media itself.

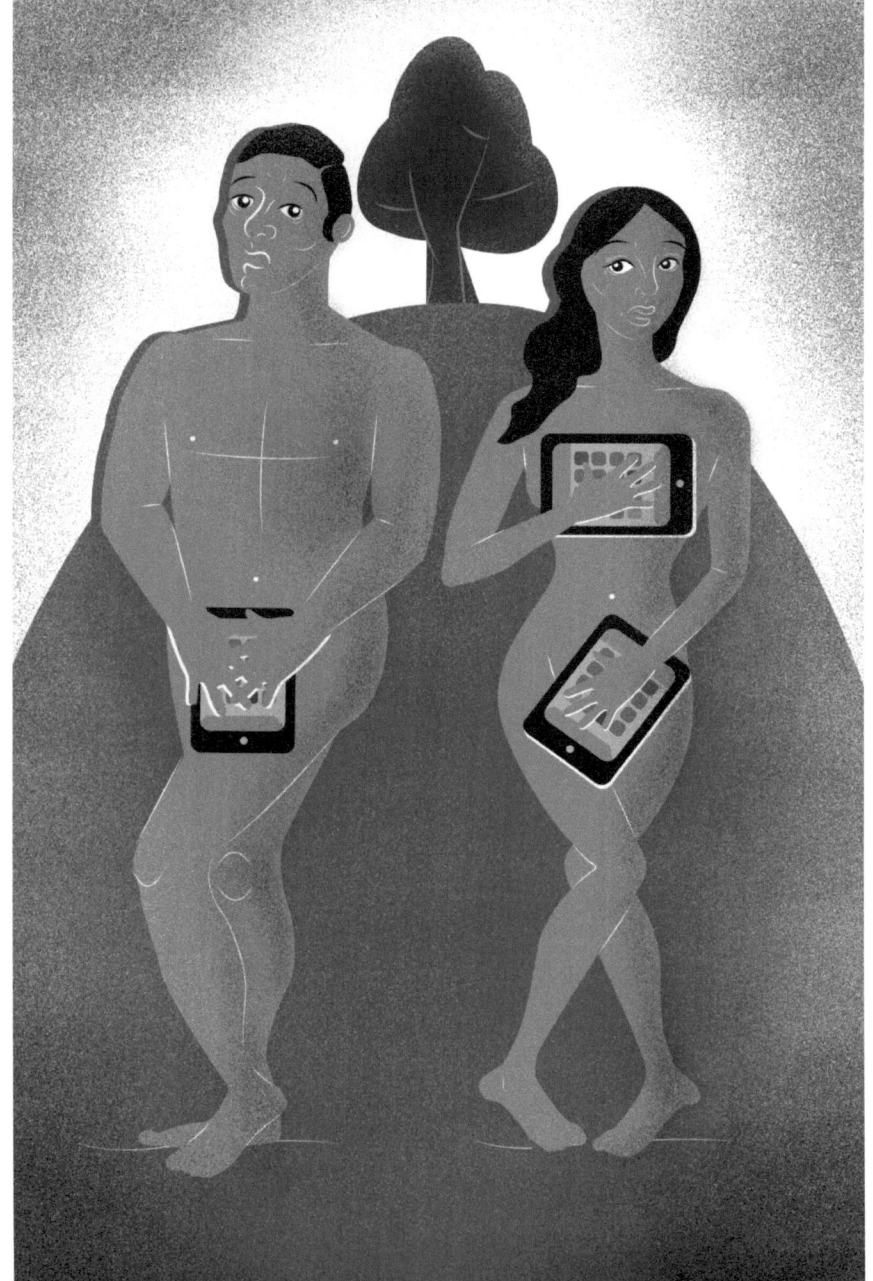

Conclusion

You Are Naked Too

I was sitting comfortably at a table at one of the many extraordinary sushi restaurants in São Paulo.

The offerings were incredible, beginning with steaming miso soup, the traditional Japanese staple that begins with the delicate dashi broth made from dried kelp. Then came charred *chu-toro*, sea bass with *shissô* (an aromatic herb), surf clam, soft octopus, exquisite yellowtail belly, sand perch and shrimp. Perfectly grilled garlic and wallops of *yuzu* make an appearance in some dishes.

Since I took a trip to Tokyo, I have been fascinated by Japanese people and their culture – especially sushi restaurants. Wanting to experience authentic Japanese sushi, I went to Liberdade, the district in São Paulo that is home to the world's largest Japanese community outside Japan.

I have tried quite a few sushi restaurants run by Japanese people, especially in London, and it's striking to me how high the standards always are. Their concern for people visiting their restaurants can't have been taught overnight. It must be in their culture. It's also their cuisine. Japan relishes its status as the nation with thirty-two three-starred Michelin restaurants, the most of any nation in the world. Thirteen are in Tokyo alone, beating Paris with its ten. After Paris comes another Japanese city, Kyoto, which is tied with New York at seven.

It must have something to do with their *kaizen*. It's Japanese for "good change," or perhaps more precisely when applied to business, "continuous improvement." *Kaizen* encompasses both productivity improvement and the humanising of the workplace, in which every worker is empowered to contribute to improvement and add value in all business processes. The practice nurtures the company's human resources and recognises the value of workers in identifying and implementing improvements. Employees from the boardroom to the customer service desk participate in *kaizen*, as well as external stakeholders when applicable. Most people know the concept of *kaizen* through the Toyota Production System (TPS), whose main objectives are to eliminate human overburden (*muri*), inconsistency (*mura*), and waste (*muda*).

Sitting at a table in the Japanese restaurant in Liberdade, I feel I'm the centre of attention. The entire experience is pleasurable – the tasteful décor, the appetising aromas of the sauces and cooking smells, the hushed attentiveness of the servers as they glided from table to table. The Japanese respect the fact that no matter how fast technology may change, there are certain fundamental values that don't change: when shopping, buying a car, or eating in a restaurant, the customer wants to feel appreciated, have a pleasing sensory experience, and be on the receiving end of kindness and enthusiasm.

In a Japanese restaurant, you feel like tipping them a lot. But you can't. They refuse to accept tips. Their kindness is simply something they do for the love of serving others. We see the opposite in the US where earnings often depend on tips based on how well your service was given. You can often spot a sincere smile, where you smile with your eyes. Love and money shouldn't be mixed.

It was the same thing I had felt during my conversations when interviewing Eloi and his company – the upholding of traditional values like good personal relation-ships, respect, and people skills that so many companies have forgotten. But in São Paulo I didn't just rediscover what worked but had been forgotten; I also discovered what the world had not seen before – how marketing can transcend and turn into a movement.

There is a reason why the Peter's bike movement has become so successful. There is something else at play here than you can't possible understand using traditional marketing concepts. It was codified by Simon Sinek at a TED talk. The movement follows the exact same pattern as other successful movements. It's the perfect example of the power of meaning and emotions. It's your purpose, your why, your cause, and your belief. The bank in São Paulo created all that through their bike project.

People don't buy what you do; they buy why you do it. This is based in the science of biology. Our newest brain, our neocortex, is responsible for all our rational thoughts but our old brain, the limbic brain, is respon-sible for all our emotions and behaviour – and that part doesn't understand reason.

Also based in biology is the human hormone oxytocin, often referred to as the "bonding hormone." Acts of human generosity release oxytocin, and it makes us feel good. But oxytocin will not be released by sending an email. Only real relations between people and people can do that.

In a naked world the impact is much greater than people might believe. This is not just a change in marketing, but also how we behave as humans making everyday decisions.

Let's say you're going out to a restaurant tonight. You and your companion – spouse, friend, business associate – are feeling adventurous and want to try some place new. You're looking for excitement, delicious food, and a memorable experience.

You see an advertisement for a restaurant. It's a slick pitch. The place looks good. You think maybe you should try it, but an inner voice says, "Make a phone call. Get some opinions."

You call your best friend. She says, "Are you kidding? I wouldn't go there even if you paid me. The food is terrible. The service is lousy."

Then she mentions another restaurant. You've never heard of it before because they don't advertise. But your friend is enthusiastic. "It's an amazing restaurant. An experience you won't forget. The chef has even written a cookbook teaching you how to make some of the restaurant's delicious dishes, you can borrow it from me if you like," she says. "The restaurant is out of the way – you would never know it was there unless you looked for it. But everyone loves it. Let's call for a reservation!"

Two businesses. In this example they're restaurants, but they could be any business – bank, car company, phone company, clothes retailer. One company buys slick ads and tries to hide behind an expensive marketing campaign. The other is "naked." It buys no traditional advertising. It relies on word of mouth and its own record of community involvement. Its marketing is transparent and interactive. It doesn't preach to its customers; it listens to them. To use an old-fashioned phrase, it lets its products and services speak for themselves.

Naked marketing provides a powerful alternative to the old-school methods of one-way broadcast advertising. There are many more ways both to engage your market and to spend your marketing money – ways that can bring your customers closer to you and make your brand a part of their lives in a way that's organic and even collaborative.

In a transparent world, we are all naked. The old guard, the people who prefer to repeat what might have worked yesterday, will face a new paradigm that some of them probably cannot adapt to. But it's going to be a better world. In a transparent world no one can lie. Companies will be more responsible and honest. And when more banks start investing in bikes for the public, we're going to have better lives.

Of the one hundred biggest economies in the world, sixty of them are not nations: They are corporations. A change in the corporate world might be the best way to change the whole world.

São Paulo showed the rest of the world how empty words on a billboard could be transformed to something much more and actually change a city. It was a win-win for its people and the companies that dared to go new ways.

It's a movement. But people need to move it. There are still too many business managers who are afraid of challenging the status quo and instead run their businesses and divisions in the safest possible manner. And there are too many numbers guys who look only at creating short-term shareholder value. Are you ready to be naked? Do you have anything to hide?

Postscript

As for me, my visit to São Paulo came to an end and it was time to go back to Denmark. I checked my flight ticket on the internet. Mysteriously, the São Paulo Frankfurt flight had disappeared. I became worried. I visited the ticket office of TAM Airlines – it's the biggest carrier in Brazil – to correct what must have been an error. Without smiling or showing any empathy, the assistant said it was cancelled! Since I didn't use the outbound ticket, they assumed I wouldn't use my inbound ticket.

She explained to me the system automatically did that. As a matter of fact, she tried to blame the system until I made a point of telling her that *people* made the system. *Her* people.

The black and white science fiction film *Alphaville* suddenly seemed too real.

She reacted like a computer would, especially when she told me the price for the so-called "no-show" fee. The inbound ticket was now more than double the price of what the whole trip had cost me. Of course this was written in very fine print somewhere on seven pages of "terms and conditions" I could have read when I bought the ticket on the internet. They were even kind enough to print it out so I could look for myself, as if it were my fault I didn't hire a lawyer to go through the sales agreement.

If this were a relationship, someone would probably say, "Why are you hiding something from me?" When the respect is gone, the love is gone. It's quite easy to see what happened here. Probably a CFO saw a tidy profit from introducing this fee. Maybe in the short term, but in the long term they lost me as a client for life; and I will never again recommend TAM Airlines to anybody. Instead they can now spend money recruiting a new customer.

And now, they are naked too. People talk, and some even write books.

It all starts with loving the customer. Just making them momentarily satisfied is not the whole answer. Go home to your own husband or spouse and say you are "satisfied" with them and see what happens.

After I flew home I found quite a few more corporations have already started and are showing the rest of us the way. This transformation is going much faster than people imagine. People are talking and recommending their shopping experiences and companies and thought leaders are also sharing their ideas. With the boom in digital technology, it's spreading like wildfire around the globe from America and Europe to the Far East and Asia. Today ideas spread faster than the flight I took across the Atlantic.

Patagonia's DamNation

We're not talking about a complete abandonment of traditional media forms, but a re-imagining of them. Sometimes a TV ad or a film can inspire, win awards, and help support a movement. It's what Patagonia, the clothing company based in California, did with their marketing dollars. The company underwrote a documentary film calling for the removal of "high cost, low value" dams along the nation's rivers and waterways. Entitled *DamNation*, the company's first foray into film production boosted Patagonia's activism to a higher level, and its release will be linked to a petition urging the federal government to tear down what Patagonia calls "deadbeat dams." The film has already inspired 25,000 people to sign the petition, and more are signing every day.

The movie's on-screen supporters, who include former US Secretary of the Interior Bruce Babbitt, advocate letting newly unstopped rivers follow their natural courses. For example, *DamNation* chronicles how quickly Chinook salmon return after the massive Elwha Dam in the US state of Washington had been demolished.

The film is not a traditional commercial; it's a statement of what Patagonia believes about the environment and a way to use the company's influence of doing good, whose clothing consumers would be proud to wear and identify with.

Shokubutsu Hana's Grass Island

Even the concept of the lowly billboard can be re- imagined. Instead of buying a traditional billboard, Japan-based natural cosmetics company Shokubutsu Hana installed toxin-absorbing grass to both create a traditional message and help clean a heavily polluted river in the Philippines. Due to negligence and industrial development, the urban waterway has become very polluted and is considered dead by ecologists. The floating arrangement of letters, which spells out "clean river soon," is made of vetiver, a type of grass that is used for treating wastewater. Shokubutsu Hana estimates the billboard cleans between 2,000 and 8,000 gallons of water per day.

The lesson: You have an opportunity to do something good for your community. But it's not only the right thing to do; it's a better investment in word of mouth, in future customer relationships, and in your reputation.

In Contrast: LEGO and McDonald's

Let's take the Danish toymaker LEGO and fast food giant McDonald's and contrast their marketing approaches. McDonald's is the most valued fast food brand in the world, while LEGO is the most valued toy brand in the world. Each year, McDonald's spends nearly one billion dollars on marketing. That means one out of every six dollars spent on restaurant advertising in America is done by McDonald's. Their goal? To make McDonald's part of the fabric of your life. To make it ubiquitous. Everywhere you go in America – and increasingly around the globe – you see McDonald's highway billboard signs, magazine ads, YouTube videos, TV commercials, movie product placements, and more. They're all an unavoidable part of peoples' daily experiences.

It's money they have to spend every year to keep people aware of them.

On the other hand, LEGO lets their customers do the talking. Actually, "fans" is a better word. There are *thirty thousand* LEGO videos on YouTube. Many of them have millions of viewers, and it's nearly all done by the community, not an advertising agency that was paid to do it.

In 2012, McDonald's tried to get its customers to talk about them. The fast food giant launched a Twitter campaign using the hashtag #McDStories. The company hoped that the hashtag would inspire its customers to post heart-warming stories about their Happy Meals and super-sized fries. The idea backfired. Customers and even McDonald's employees posted snarky tweets, turning it into a #bashtag to share their #McDHorrorStories.

The bad news spread incredibly fast. The *Los Angeles Times* reported that the company pulled the campaign within *two hours* of its launch. But they discovered crowd-sourced campaigns are hard to stop, and the #McDStories hashtag persisted.

While McDonald's is there to earn money for its shareholders, the family-owned LEGO wants to "inspire and develop the builders of tomorrow." Where would you prefer to work? Maybe your company is not like McDonald's, but do your customers talk about you and your products like they do about LEGO?

You Can Start Today

As we've seen, even a bank can redefine itself and start a movement. How can you redefine your business? What movement would you start?

Start by listening to what your customers are saying. Figure out how you can make their lives a bit better. Maybe you can't afford a thousand bikes for the public, or it doesn't make sense for your business, but maybe you can teach your potential customers something. Teaching, giving, and sharing are very effective ways to engage people. You need to touch them on a personal level. Either on the phone next time you give them advice or when you start a social project, you will gain respect and people will start listening to you. Suddenly you're not boring anymore. Because you have given them something of value, they might even tell that to their friends. Pitching or selling will never be shared. Instead, stand out and be remembered.

Will you be remembered if suddenly you're not here anymore? If you swap jobs or the day comes when you'll inevitably retire, will you be missed? Maybe you won't put a ding in the universe like Steve Jobs. But maybe you could reach your customers, colleagues, and community, and make them feel good. Make them smile. And when they smile, you will smile too. It's that simple. And if you start today, maybe one day you will leave a legacy.

It's easier to stand out than you think. We have become so used to disengaged customer service that we see it as normal. Creating that customer experience through either your service or social project will be appreciated by people, and they will be ready to thank you when you make their lives better.

One day the bank will teach the entrepreneur to grow its business.

One day your customer will become a person you want to help – even after they step out of your shop.

One day you will earn your bonus not by how many new clients you attract but by how many you make happy.

One day there will be no space for advertising, only space for conversation where people are talking about you.

One day is today.

How do your clients look at you?

Do you clients consider you one among a number of unimportant suppliers with which they do business and will eventually replace with someone else?

How many of your clients will recommend you?

If you want to start listening to your clients and challenge status quo, contact us for a talk with a real person at Relationwise.

Contact us at info@relationwise.com

Recommended

Be the company people ♥ to recommend

How?

The book Naked Marketing will tell you WHY it is more important today than ever before to redefine your understanding of marketing.

But HOW can you do this – and how do you create growth by marketing your business in a new way? You can read about this in the book Recommended. The book will teach you, step by step, how you make your clients love your company and recommend it to others. You will learn that happy clients are a good thing – it is just not enough.

The book contains inspiring case stories and theoretical reflections, which will give you unique insight into some companies' visionary view upon their clients – a view that has placed them among the world's leading.

Download Recommended (PDF file) free of charge at www.relationwise.com